D0598333

COOL

JOBS

for

Kids Who Like Kids

Ways to Make Money Working with Children

Pam Scheunemann

ABDO
Publishing Company

Visit us at www.abdopublishing.com

Published by ABDO Publishing Company, 8000 West 78th Street, Edina, Minnesota 55439.
Copyright © 2011 by Abdo Consulting Group, Inc. International copyrights reserved in all countries.
No part of this book may be reproduced in any form without written permission from the publisher.
The Checkerboard Library™ is a trademark and logo of ABDO Publishing Company.

Printed in the United States , North Mankato, Minnesota
052010
092010

Design and Production: Kelly Doudna, Mighty Media, Inc.
Series Editor: Liz Salzmann
Photo Credits: Kelly Doudna, iStockPhoto (Randy Plett Photographs), Shutterstock
Money Savvy Pig® photo courtesy of Money Savvy Generation/www.msgen.com

**Library of Congress
Cataloging-in-Publication Data**

Scheunemann, Pam, 1955-
  Cool jobs for kids who like kids : ways to make money working with children / Pam Scheunemann.
    p. cm. -- (Cool kid jobs)
  Includes index.
  ISBN 978-1-61613-196-8   4565 7672 5/11
  1. Money-making projects for children--Juvenile literature.
2. Child care--Vocational guidance--Juvenile literature. 3.
Success in business--Juvenile literature. 4. Finance, Personal
--Juvenile literature. I. Title.
  HF5392.S34 2011
  331.702--dc22
                            2010004313

NOTE TO ADULTS

A job can be a good learning experience for you and your child. Be sure to encourage your child to discuss his or her job ideas with you. Talk about the risks and the benefits. Set up some rules for your child's safety with regard to:

* working with strangers

* transportation to and from the job

* proper and safe use of tools or equipment

* giving out phone numbers or e-mail addresses

* emergency contacts

Contents

Why Work?

There are a lot of reasons to have a job. The first one you probably think of is to earn money. But you can get more out of a job than just money. You can learn new skills, meet new people, and get some experience.

MAKING MONEY

When you do a job such as helping take care of kids, you are providing a service. If people pay you for your service, you can earn some money!

BESIDES MONEY

You will gain more than money from having a job. You also get work experience and learn about being responsible. That means showing up on time, keeping your word, and being trustworthy.

Volunteering is doing a job you don't get paid for. But you can earn other rewards. You can learn new skills that will help you get other jobs. And you can feel good about helping out!

What Can You Do with Your Money?

There are four things you can do with the money you earn.

SAVE

Saving is keeping your money in a safe place. You add money a little at a time as you earn it. Soon you could save enough for something such as a new bike.

SPEND

Spending is using your money to buy things you want. Maybe you want to go to a movie or buy a new computer game.

DONATE

It is important to give some of your earnings to organizations that help others.

INVEST

Investing is saving for long-term goals such as college expenses.

Ask your parents to help you decide how much money to use for each purpose. You'll be glad you did!

Money Savvy Pig®

What's Your Plan?

Each state has laws about kids working. If you are too young to work at a regular job, you can create your own job. Whatever job you try, you should have a plan.

WHAT WILL YOU DO?

Your job should relate to your abilities and likes. Make a list of the ways you know how to play with and care for kids. Which do you like doing the most? That's a good place to start!

WHO ARE YOUR CUSTOMERS?

Who needs your product or service? Where will you find your customers? How will you let people know about your services?

WHERE WILL YOU DO THE WORK?

Will you work at your house, the customers' homes, or another location?

SETTING REALISTIC GOALS

A goal is something you are working toward. When you set your job goals, keep these things in mind:

* Do you have permission from your parents?

* Is your idea something you already know how to do?

* Will this job interfere with your schoolwork or other activities?

* Are there any costs to start your job? Do you have the money or do you need to get a loan?

* Are there tools or **materials** you need to start your job? Will you continue to need supplies?

* Will you work alone or with a friend? How will you divide the work and the money you make?

What If It Doesn't Work?

Don't get **discouraged** if things don't work out the way you planned. Think about what you could have done differently and try again!

WELCOME TO THE THEATER!

Get Permission

You must get permission from a parent or **guardian** before you work for someone else. Give your parents all of the **details** about the job.

WHO WILL YOU BE WORKING FOR?

Are you working for a relative or friend of the family? If not, your parents should meet your customer.

WHEN WILL YOU BE WORKING?

What day will you start the work? What time? Will your services be needed once or more often?

WHERE IS THE JOB?

Be sure your family has the address and phone number of where you are working. Create a Customer Information form similar to the one on page 15. Fill out a form for each customer.

HOW WILL YOU GET THERE?

Is your job within walking or biking distance? Do you need a ride there? Is it okay for you to take the bus to get there? What if it's during the evening or after dark?

WHO ELSE WILL BE THERE?

Are you going to do the job alone or with a friend? Will there be other people around while you are working?

WHAT IS EXPECTED OF YOU?

Are you clear about the job you were hired to do? Have you made an agreement with the customer about what is expected of you (see page 14)?

Be Smart, Be Safe

Talk with your parents about working for strangers. Always tell your parents where you are going and what time they should expect you to be home. Make sure they have a phone number where they can reach you while you are working.

CHILDREN'S SAFETY

When you watch little kids, you are responsible for keeping them safe. That means you need to know where they are at all times. Also, be sure you know what they are doing. There are many everyday things that can be harmful to children. You need to be aware of all the dangers.

It is important to know how to get help in case of any **emergency**. Make sure you have a way to contact the child's parents if necessary.

Getting the Word Out

Okay, you've decided what to do. Now how do you get the work? There are different ways to get the word out.

BUSINESS CARDS

A simple business card can be very helpful in getting customers. Give cards to the people you talk to about your business. Maybe even give each person an extra so he or she can pass one along to a friend.

Your business card should have your name, your business name, and your phone number. Get permission from a parent before putting your home address, phone number, or e-mail address on a card.

WORD OF MOUTH

Let as many people know about your business as you can. They'll tell other people, and those people will tell more people, and so on.

Child's Play Craft Club

Ron and Angie Smith
1234 Anystreet
Dallas, TX 59404
(214) 555-0164

Make Your Own Business Cards

1 On a piece of white paper, draw a rectangle with a black pen. It should be 3½ x 2 inches (9 x 5 cm). Design your business card inside the rectangle.

2 Make 11 copies of the card. Cut each one out, including the original. Cut outside the border so the lines show.

3 Tape the cards onto a piece of 8½ x 11-inch (22 x 28 cm) paper. Leave a ¼-inch (½ cm) border around the edge of the paper. This is your business card **master**.

4 Copy the master onto card stock. If you're using a black-and-white copier, try using colored card stock. Or, use white card stock and add color with markers or colored pencils.

5 Cut out your business cards. When you run out of cards, make more copies of your master.

PRO TIP
Use the computer to make your flyer and cards. Or, follow the steps here and on page 13 for a more personal touch.

WHAT YOU'LL NEED

white paper
ruler
black pen
copier
scissors

tape
card stock (white or colored)
markers or colored pencils

Child's Play Craft Club

Ron and Angie Smith
1234 Any Street
Dallas, TX 59404
(214) 555-0164

Child's Play Craft Club

Get your child involved!

The Child's Play Craft Club makes crafts fun for kids ages 4 to 8.

The club meets Tuesdays from 4:00–6:00 and Saturdays from 10:00–Noon.

Parents can leave their kids for a couple of hours. Kids will have fun making really cool stuff!

Kids will get to:
- Paint
- Draw
- Color
- Make sculptures
- And more!

Sign up your child now!
For more information
call Ron Smith or Angie Smith
at (214) 555-0164

Child's Play Craft Club
(214) 555-0164

A flyer is a one-page sheet about your product or service. You can include more information than will fit on a business card. Make little mini cards at the bottom of the flyer for people to tear off. Include your service and phone number. Get your parent's permission first! Give flyers to people you know. Also, some places have bulletin boards for flyers:

* apartment building lobbies
* stores
* community centers
* schools
* places of worship

Make Your Own Flyer

1. Design a **master** copy of your flyer on a sheet of white paper that is 8½ x 11 inches (22 x 28 cm).

2. Use bright colors so your flyer will stand out. If you plan to use a black-and-white copier, use black on the master and copy it onto colored paper.

3. Remember that copiers won't copy anything written too close to the edge of the master. So leave a border of at least ¼ inch (½ cm) on all sides.

4. Make as many copies of the master as you need. Cut the lines between the mini cards so customers can tear them off easily.

WHAT YOU'LL NEED

white paper

black pen

ruler

markers or colored pencils

copier

colored paper (optional)

scissors

Money Matters

One reason to work is so you can make money!

Here are some hints about money.

Sample form: make yours fit your business!

Child's Play Craft Club Customer Agreement

Child's Name _____

Parent's Name _____

Address _____

Phone _____

April/May Attendance Schedule (check if attending)

_____ Tuesday, April 2 . . . . Materials/Snack Fee $ _____
_____ Saturday, April 6 . . . . Materials/Snack Fee $ _____
_____ Tuesday, April 9 . . . . Materials/Snack Fee $ _____
_____ Saturday, April 13 . . . . Materials/Snack Fee $ _____
_____ Tuesday, April 16 . . . . Materials/Snack Fee $ _____
_____ Saturday, April 20 . . . . Materials/Snack Fee $ _____
_____ Tuesday, April 23 . . . . Materials/Snack Fee $ _____
_____ Saturday, April 27 . . . . Materials/Snack Fee $ _____
_____ Tuesday, April 30 . . . . Sub Total $ _____

Rate/Payment Agreement

Customer agrees to pay Child's Play Craft Club $_____ for each session in addition to the materials/snack fee listed above.

Payments will be made on a [per visit, weekly, monthly] basis.

Total for Sessions: _____ Sessions @ _____ /each = $_____
Total Materials/Snack Fees $_____
TOTAL DUE $_____

Parent's Signature _____ Date _____

Child's Play Craft Club
Ron and Angie Smith, 1234 Anystreet, Dallas, TX 59404
(214) 555-0164

HOW MUCH SHOULD YOU CHARGE?

Here are things to consider when figuring out what to charge.

* Find out what other people charge for the same product or service.

* Are you providing tools or supplies? Make sure you charge enough to cover your costs.

* Do you want to charge by the hour or by the job? Will you charge less if they are steady customers?

Make an Agreement

Be clear with your customer about how much you are charging. Discuss the **details** with the customer.

Child's Play Craft Club
Customer Information

Child's Name:	
Parent's Name:	Age:
Address:	
Phone Number:	
Emergency Phone Numbers:	
Parent:	
Other Friend/Relative:	
Child's Health/Allergy Issues:	

Child's Play Craft Club
Ron and Angie Smith, 1234 Anystreet, Dallas, TX 59404
(214) 555-0164

Sample form: make yours fit your business!

Then write them down on a Customer Agreement form. You and the customer should each have a copy of the Agreement.

Fill out a Customer Information form for each customer. Keep them in a folder with the Customer Agreements. Update the forms if anything changes.

HOW MUCH
DID YOU MAKE?

Profit is the amount of money you have left after you subtract your expenses. If you are only charging for your time, it's all profit, right? Not so fast! Did you have to make flyers or business cards? Did you provide supplies to do the job?

Add up your expenses. Subtract the expenses from the amount you earned. The amount left over is your profit.

Duck, Duck Play Group

Try hosting a weekly play group. Parents can drop off their kids for some fun and games.

ACTIVITY IDEAS

seven up
duck, duck, goose
Simon says
beanbag toss
red light, green light
draw or color pictures
read stories
play cds and dance
build things with blocks

BEFORE YOU BEGIN

Think about how many kids you can handle at a time. Maybe you want to do this with a friend. Then you can entertain more kids.

Get permission from your parents to hold a play group. An adult must be around during the play group.

Decide how much to charge for each child. If you are serving a snack, include extra for that cost.

Have each child's parent fill out a Customer Information form (see page 15). Make sure the form includes spaces for:

* the parents' and child's names

* **emergency** phone numbers

* any **allergies** the child has

* other health issues that affect the child

* anything else the parents think you should know about the child

ON THE JOB

* Plan indoor and outdoor activities for each **session**. Then you'll be ready if it's too cold or rainy to go outside.

* Think about games you enjoyed playing when you were younger. Will those games work in the space you have?

* Pay equal attention to all of the kids.

* Make sure everyone plays fair and gets a turn.

* Some kids may have special needs, so take that into consideration.

* Look for books on kids' games at the library.

Make Your Own Beanbag Toss Game

Put dried beans into small zipper bags to make beanbags. Cut a hole in a cardboard box. Have the kids try to toss the beanbags into the hole.

17

Happy Helper

Many families have young children. Sometimes the parents would like someone to play with the kids. If you enjoy little kids and are too young to be a babysitter on your own, this may be the job for you!

WHAT YOU'LL NEED

toys

games

paper and crayons

children's books

BEFORE YOU BEGIN

Meet with your customer to find out about the job. Always make sure an adult will be home while you are there. Fill out a Customer Agreement form (see page 14). Write down all the **details** for the job.

Talk about how often would they like you to help out. Maybe you can set up a regular **schedule**.

Learn the rules of the house. Is a time limit on TV? Is it okay to eat in the living room?

Find out if you will need to prepare bottles or change diapers. Get instructions from the parent.

Have the parent fill out a Customer Information form (see page 15). Make sure the form includes spaces for:

* the parents' and child's names

* **emergency** phone numbers

* any **allergies** the child has

* other health issues that affect the child

* anything else the parents think you should know about the child

ON THE JOB

* Get an adult immediately if anyone gets hurt, including you.

* Kids old enough to crawl or walk can get into anything! You must watch them at all times.

* Bring a bag of games and activities with you. Kids enjoy doing new things.

* Kids like to play dress up. Ask a parent if there are dress-up clothes.

* Go to the library and find some books to read to the kids. If a child can read, let him or her read to you.

* Don't forget to clean up before you leave. Remember, you are there to help, not make more of a mess.

REUSE TOYS
Bring some of your old toys with you for the kids to play with.

Child's Play Craft Club

Kids like to be creative and make things. If you are creative too, turn your creativity into a money-making adventure!

WHAT YOU'LL NEED

Supplies for the projects

Cleaning supplies

BEFORE YOU BEGIN

Ask your parents if it's okay for you to have a weekly craft club. Be sure an adult will be home during your meetings.

Set up an area that you can use to make crafts. Save old newspapers to cover your work surface. Remember, there will be a mess!

Figure out how many kids you can fit into your craft area. Decide if you need a friend to help. That way you could have more kids.

Pick several projects you can do with the kids. Figure out how much money each project costs to do. Add a **materials** fee to the amount you charge for attendance.

Have each child's parent fill out a Customer Information form (see page 15). Make sure the form includes spaces for:

* the parents' and child's names

* **emergency** phone numbers

* any **allergies** the child has

* other health issues that affect the child

* anything else the parents think you should know about the child

ON THE JOB

* Try out new projects ahead of time. Make sure they are easy for young kids to do.

* Boys and girls like to do different types of things. If you have boys and girls in your club, have options for them to choose from.

* Have the kids bring an apron or old shirt to cover their clothes.

* Clean up after the kids have gone home. If you don't, your parents may decide you can't do it again! Be responsible.

* Research at the library, in magazines, and online for new craft ideas.

* Always use non-toxic craft supplies such as clay, paint, and glue.

FUN AND EASY CRAFTS

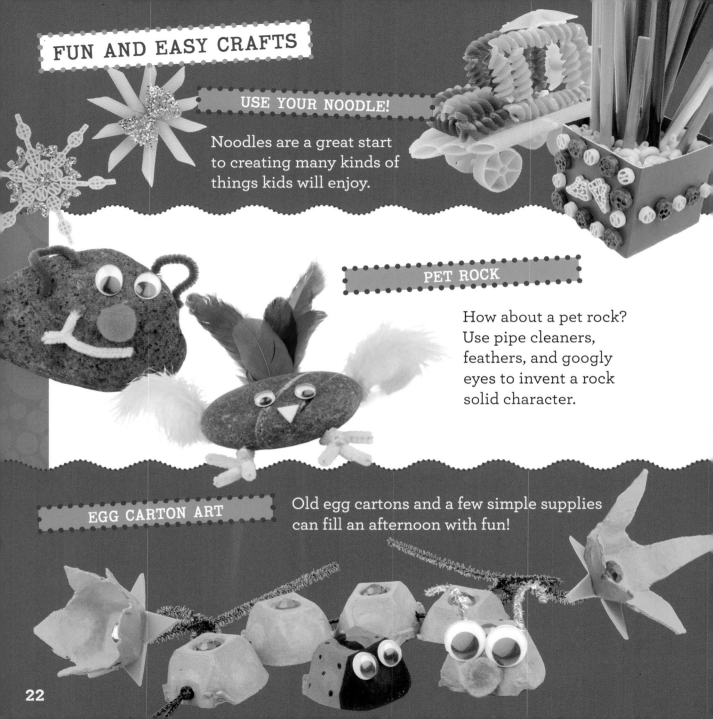

USE YOUR NOODLE!

Noodles are a great start to creating many kinds of things kids will enjoy.

PET ROCK

How about a pet rock? Use pipe cleaners, feathers, and googly eyes to invent a rock solid character.

EGG CARTON ART

Old egg cartons and a few simple supplies can fill an afternoon with fun!

Use mini cars to make a mini painting. Drive a car through stripes of paint to make tire tracks.

Put a few drops of paint on a paper plate and roll a marble around for cool patterns!

EDIBLE SCULPTURES

Find food that can be connected with stick pretzels. Let the kids go crazy!

23

Show Off Theater Group

Do you like drama, music, or dance? Do you enjoy being with little kids? If you do, this might be the business for you. You can start a neighborhood theater group!

WHAT YOU'LL NEED

- 3-panel presentation board
- ruler
- pencil
- craft knife
- paint and paintbrushes
- craft foam
- gems
- glue
- scissors
- piece of fabric
- masking tape
- old socks
- googly eyes
- felt
- yarn
- craft sticks
- pom poms
- pipe cleaners

BEFORE YOU BEGIN

Make sure you have permission to hold the theater group. Make sure an adult will be around while the group is meeting.

Find a place big enough for the group to practice and perform. Decide how often you want to have meetings. You could meet once or twice a week, or once a month. It's up to you.

Decide how much to charge for each child who joins. When you set the fee, think about the cost of **materials** and any snacks you plan to serve.

Make a flyer to advertise your theater group. Put copies around your neighborhood.

Have each child's parent fill out a Customer Information form (see page 15). Make sure the form includes spaces for:

* the parents' and child's names

* **emergency** phone numbers

* any **allergies** the child has

* other health issues that affect the child

* anything else the parents think you should know about the child

ON THE JOB

Decide what type of performance will work for your group. Select one that fits the ages of the kids in your group. Make sure it's something that they'll all enjoy.

* Have the kids dance or sing to different types of music.

* The kids could act out a story as you read it.

* Do a **puppet** show and make all your own puppets. You can make the stage out of a three-**panel** presentation board!

* Put on a talent show. Each act can be something different. Act one could be a dance. Act two could be a song. Act three could be a **skit**.

* Go to the library and look for stories, music, or other performance ideas.

MAKE YOUR OWN PUPPET THEATER

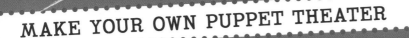

Use simple art **materials** to make **puppets**.
Kids will enjoy making their own characters!

MAKE THE PUPPETS

You may want to make a couple of examples to get the kids started. Encourage them to use their imaginations to come up with interesting characters.

Set out a bunch of supplies for the kids to use.

Socks are an easy way to make fun puppets. Glue on googly eyes. Cut shapes out of felt for noses, tongues, and ears. You could add some yarn hair.

Craft sticks can be used to make many different kinds of puppets. Glue on pom poms, googly eyes, craft foam, gems, or anything else that works for the characters.

Pipe cleaners are easy to twist into butterflies or other crazy critters.

With a ruler and a pencil, draw a rectangle near the top of the center **panel** of the presentation board. It should be almost as wide as the panel. This will be the stage. Have an adult help you cut out the rectangle with a craft knife.

Paint the board. You could make each panel a different color. Or the ends could be a different color than the middle.

Draw a frame around the stage and paint it a different color than the background. Write the name of your group or theater on the stage.

Have the kids help decorate the board. Use paint, craft foam, gems, or other decorations.

Cut a piece of fabric a little larger than the stage opening. Place it over the back of the stage opening. Put masking tape along the top of the fabric to attach it to the board. This is the backdrop.

Show the kids how to use **puppets** from behind the board. The kids sit or kneel so they are below the stage. They hold the puppets up in front of the backdrop.

PROP TIP
Look around the house for things to use for props and costumes. Ask the kids to bring in old clothes.

Coach's Helper

Most communities have sports teams for kids. If you like sports, you could try being a coach's helper.

Find a team that you are not playing on. It could be a team for younger or older kids. Ask the coach if he or she will hire you to help out. The coach may be able to pay you. Or you might be a **volunteer**.

Fill out a Customer Agreement form (see page 14). Write down all the **details** for the job.

Discuss with the coach what your duties would be. Whether you are being paid or not, you need to be responsible. That means showing up on time and doing the best you can.

Get the practice and game **schedules** from the coach.

Make sure you have a way to get to the practices and games. Will a parent drive you or can you ride with someone? Where would you meet the coach? Is it okay with your parents?

SAVE UP!
You can save any money you earn to buy your own sports equipment!

ON THE JOB

* Your job will be easier if you know about the sport. If you don't already know about it, research it. Learn the rules and coaching methods. You can find this information online or at the library.

* Learn about the equipment. Know what it's for and how to care for it. Know where it gets put away.

* If you are helping keep score, pay attention to the game. The teams are counting on you to get it right!

* Be sure to wear the proper clothing. If the game is outside, dress for the weather. Make sure you won't get too cold or wet.

* Know where to find the first aid kit at all times.

* Be a good sport. That's important for any sport or game.

Tips for Success

Success isn't measured just by how much money you make. How you look and behave is also important.

BE ON TIME

Show that you are responsible and follow through on your agreements.

BE POLITE

This means that you need to respect your customer. Do not interrupt. Ask any questions politely. Be respectful even if you don't agree with someone.

DRESS FOR THE JOB

Be neat and clean, even if it's a dirty job! Wear the right clothing for the job.

BE ON THE SAFE SIDE

Follow safety instructions. Review tool or equipment safety before you start a job. Never try to use a tool or machine that you are not familiar with. Always have **emergency** contact information.

ALWAYS COMPLETE THE JOB

Remember the agreement you made? You need to follow through and do everything you agreed to do. Put away all tools and supplies you use. If you are messy or don't finish a job, you probably won't be hired again!

THIS IS JUST THE BEGINNING

Okay, it is the end of the book. But, it is just the beginning for you! This book has provided information about some ways to make money. Now decide what might work for you. Talk it over with your parents. And don't forget to have fun!

Glossary

allergy – an unpleasant reaction after eating, touching, or breathing something.

detail – a small part of something.

discouraged – feeling that you can't do something, or that something isn't worth trying.

emergency – a sudden, unexpected, dangerous situation that requires immediate attention.

guardian – the person who, by law, cares for a minor.

master – an original copy that is reproduced to make more of the same thing.

material – the substance something is made of, such as metal, fabric, or plastic.

panel – part of a flat surface such as a wall or screen.

puppet – a doll that can be moved by strings, a stick, or a hand placed inside it.

schedule – a list of the times when things will happen.

session – a period of time used for a specific purpose or activity.

skit – a short performance that is usually funny.

volunteer – 1. to offer to do a job, most often without pay. 2. a person who offers to do a job, most often without pay.

WEB SITES

To learn more about the jobs that kids can do, visit ABDO Publishing Company on the World Wide Web at www.abdopublishing.com. Web sites about creative ways for kids to earn money are featured on our Book Links page. These links are routinely monitored and updated to provide the most current information available.

Index